Celebrating Differences

Different Interests

by Rebecca Pettiford

Bullfrog Books

Ideas for Parents and Teachers

Bullfrog Books let children practice reading informational text at the earliest reading levels. Repetition, familiar words, and photo labels support early readers.

Before Reading

- Discuss the cover photo. What does it tell them?

- Look at the picture glossary together. Read and discuss the words.

Read the Book

- "Walk" through the book and look at the photos. Let the child ask questions. Point out the photo labels.

- Read the book to the child, or have him or her read independently.

After Reading

- Prompt the child to think more. Ask: Think about some of the activities your friends enjoy. Do you they have any hobbies you'd like to learn? Do you have any hobbies you'd enjoy sharing with them?

Bullfrog Books are published by Jump!
5357 Penn Avenue South
Minneapolis, MN 55419
www.jumplibrary.com

Library of Congress Cataloging-in-Publication Data

Names: Pettiford, Rebecca, author.
Title: Different interests / by Rebecca Pettiford.
Description: Minneapolis, MN: Jump!, Inc., [2018]
Series: Celebrating differences | Published also in Spanish. | Includes index. | Description based on print version record and CIP data provided by publisher; resource not viewed.
Identifiers: LCCN 2016055047 (print)
LCCN 2017011469 (ebook)
ISBN 9781624965487 (ebook)
ISBN 9781620316719 (hardcover : alk. paper)
ISBN 9781620317242 (pbk.)
Subjects: LCSH: Hobbies—Juvenile literature.
Classification: LCC GV1201.5 (ebook)
LCC GV1201.5 P48 2017 (print) | DDC 790.1/3—dc23
LC record available at https://lccn.loc.gov/2016055047

Editor: Jenny Fretland VanVoorst
Book Designer: Leah Sanders
Photo Researcher: Leah Sanders

Photo Credits: Alamy: Leila Cutler, 12–13. Getty: Ronnie Kaufman/Larry Hirshowitz, 5; Hero Images, 6–7; Jamie Grill, 8–9; Steve Debenport, 14; Mikael Vaisanen, 16–17; Don Mason, 17; Jon Feingersh, 19. iStock: monkeybusinessimages, 4; yenwen, 18. Shutterstock: Sergiy Bykhunenko, 1; Pete Pahham, 3; fotoinfot, 10–11; Brandelet, 15; VisanuPhotoshop, 22tl; Ilike, 22tm; Dragon Images, 22tr; Maria Uspenskaya, 22ml; pirita, 22m; Africa Studio, 22mr; CREATISTA, 22bl; Dreams Come True, 22bm; Tomsickova Tatyana, 22br; Patrick Foto, 24.

Printed in the United States of America at Corporate Graphics in North Mankato, Minnesota.

Table of Contents

What Do You Do?

We all like to do different things.

Sam likes to cook.

His dad helps.

Jim and Bri like to sew.

What are they making?

A surprise for Dad!

Ben likes to read.

Look at all his books!

Kay likes judo.
She practices
with a friend.

Jack is making a pot.

He uses clay.

It looks messy.

It looks fun!

Some people have fun outside.

Fran likes to fish.

Lucy climbs a rock.

bow

arrows

Petra is an archer.

She draws her bow.

Her arrow flies.

Look! She hit
her mark!

Joy likes to garden.

Cam likes to draw.

What do you like to do?

So Many Interests

There are so many things people like to do. Look at the pictures of kids having fun. Which of these activities have you tried? Which would you like to try?

Picture Glossary

 **archer**
A person who uses a bow and arrow to hit a target.

 **judo**
A sport in which two people try to throw each other to the ground.

 **garden**
To plant seeds and care for them as they grow.

 **sew**
To fix or make things out of fabric using a needle and thread.

Index

To Learn More

Learning more is as easy as 1, 2, 3.

1) Go to www.factsurfer.com

2) Enter "differentinterests" into the search box.

3) Click the "Surf" button to see a list of websites.

With factsurfer.com, finding more information is just a click away.